ARGUMENT

FOR

LOVE

POEMS BY JAMES HUMPHREY

This first edition of *ARGUMENT FOR LOVE* consists of 1,500 copies of which 100 are numbered & signed by the poet

ARGUMENT FOR LOVE

Poems By James Humphrey

KENDALL

My thanks are given to the editors
of the following publications in which
some of these poems first appeared:

*SUMAC; PENUMBRA; captain may i;
SUCTION; CRONOPIOUS; THE IOWA DEFENDER;
BONES; TENTACLE; IOWA ARTS COUNCIL
NEWSLETTER; ABRAXAS; CRUCIBLE*

The poem *ARGUMENT FOR LOVE* was written
in Marshalltown, Iowa, during January 1969.

To Norma, Saroyan,
& our 1956 Oldsmobile

CONTENTS

ARGUMENT FOR LOVE

WE ARE

We are
under one roof
lying in the big soft
bed looking up into
Our Heaven
that will last
for awhile because
we are
human & have differences.

QUESTION

She knows
if she tries

it will make
a difference. But think,

dear: in which direction,
for what reason.

WHERE I WAS

There is nothing
to turn to, but
I must watch
thinking, hopefully,
in the midst of
senseless ears
for, if nothing else,
a way through or out

to the wind
as blow around me
as not, but harmless

FOUND

You knew
the sun
as light on you
as anyone
took me in
between
your lovely legs;
coming up, over
around me
knocking me senseless;
relieved: the rhythm
of myself returning
again

HER LOVE
for Kirstin Sonstegard

In love's body
she stands
at the window

brushing her long
hair through the new
morning's sunshine

humming to him,
still sleeping,
a private rhythm.

FOR LOVE

I stole some broom-
straw flowers from
you while you were

taking a shower and
hid them in my suit-
case, not feeling the

guilt I had
been taught since child-
hood to feel for

stealing. For many years
I was obedient, mother,
teachers, books and priests

but somewhere, sometime,
for some reason for-
gotten now, I tried to

define stealing.
I
could-

'nt. Humphrey says:
it's better to steal
from each other now
and then than to
reach   out
for   purity and
die in fantasy.

AT DAWN   4-10-69

to the sound of the day
waking up
          as they say   (in the cold
light of dawn)
money is it or songs to sings

What could you show me I did not know
until your yellow dress I might spread
on the soft damp grass,
tenderly:
"it's cold
& I'm only passing"   she said

SOMETIMES

Snow is melting
on the sidewalk
you walk on, passing
me at my writing table

just sitting there
looking out.
Would you go to bed
with me if I asked

you? Of course, you have
dishes to do. I want
to marry your body
so I can write poems

again. Do you understand
that? For a moment
I realize how good it
would be with you. I

will show you. Step in
a puddle, throw a snow ball,
bring some reality into
your life before you've

passed behind me. Some-
times it's just there
through the window, watching,
trusting my sanity.

POEM

The reflection is green
in the window
from a candle
in a green glass jar
setting on a surface,
probably wooden,
against a wall
that is light coloured,
probably white,
in the room
where I am sitting
in a chair
at a table

ALL

All there was
left,
was all there
was: days
that killed
you; all one,
to this
way with
us:
two
at the moment
at once.
Years since,
you said.
Here,
somewhere
taking shape:
don't stop
now

THE FIRST TIME

Slowly,
for the first time

ever,
she was satisfied;

almost saying, oh,
through his patient sweat.

CAMPING TRIP

Getting into myself
was knowing
the mosquitoes were

real; paddling
on air mattresses
in the lake was

feeling
myself
touching you:

singing out
that night
in the tent

before the wine,
I love you:
fully feeling

TWO

She, from
back in there,
in a moment,
saw
mother's way
pulling against her;
said
I don't know
where I am,
when my sperm,
high inside her,
screamed to know
the time too

RELIEF IN A SIMPLE RECOGNITION

Sitting on the edge of the bed:
A little like a girl, her hole was tight,
that's all. Dress. Leave.
Made it. Barely. But made it.

GETTING UP

There's still something about blond brides
in white that turns me on when

I'm flat on my back

PURITAN ETHICS
BLOND PRINCESSES IN THE NURSERY STORIES
UNITED WE STAND
NOW YOU CAN BE AN INNOCENT BLOND AGAIN
FROM CLAIROL

"There's alot of Bastards out there."

Joseph Conrad said that

Sitting on the floor now   Inhale   Exhale
check for cigarettes, matches
OK   lite up
did it.

I won't let anybody bury me
'on the lone prayer-ee.'   Getting up
Thanks Joe.

AFTER BUYING A NEW
TYPEWRITER RIBBON
for Norma

Necessity
found us
at the gas station
this way; you
behind the door
marked LADIES
& me behind
the one marked
MEN, stealing
toilet paper & light
bulbs so I could
buy a new typewriter
ribbon & see
this black ink
again

3 POEMS FOR CHRISTMAS OR
I BELIEVE IN THE TRINITY

1

In a week is the 25th
of Dec. My son & I are
going to slide on his sled
I stole from a front-yard
yesterday at 5 A.M. when I
was walking home drunk
after my car wouldn't
start.

2

You are with me
always, in my head
where it all is when
the distance is unknown
to where you are.

For Christmas I mailed
you a Greyhound bus air-
mail, special delivery
to our old address with
the note, "If you look
through the window, you can
see me," and asked a poet
to drink to the last
Greyhound he sees while he
is hitch-hiking to Rhode
Island to make new
memories with his love.

3

Christmas Is
for sale.

AGAIN

Coming to or what-
ever it's called the next
day after a hard

drunk, I opened my
eyes and tried to bring
something back from

it. Couldn't. So I
rolled over to sleep
into it or away,

which ever way sleep
took me, and saw
a new girl beside me

smiling the smile
a girl smiles at you
when it's been good.

I smile your smile
back, knowing it
all now.

SNOW ANGELS

There
in the new snow

we laid down
on our backs, reaching

out; our legs
spreading, the arms

moving out, up
touching the hands

at the top; knowing
how I am with you

is only to the extent
that I know you;

rolling to our sides,
falling forward

in an easy grace
to love against

my parka under
your goose-bumped

bottom: creating
patterns children won't

question and adults
will never see.

TODAY

Today I am
looking out
all around
me: I am

all that I am.
Rejoice if I love
you. It is the best
of my love.
I am I.

PERSONAL POEM #1

There is no point
to believe
you are my life.
How nice
before I die,
loving you
without asking

PERSONAL POEM #3

When there's no food
I make a can of beer last
five hours when I'm writing
poetry. When there's no food
or beer, I prepare myself
for the poems I'll write
when there's food or beer

LOVE WITH NUMBERS
                    for Robert Creeley

One wants one
to have two.
Two wants one
but three, too.
Three wants
two not one;
so one finds another
one who wants one
one, leaving two and three
                two and three or
                four and six
but not two and
two and three and three.

HOW LIKE YOU

How like you
a sudden flash
of light passes
quickly

Across
the bed
you sleep
to yourself

Turtles too,
lay eggs

Love them all
but keep a home
in your mind:

I hold my son's
hand when I'm
climbing stairs

Sweet breath
of clarity

PROSTITUTE

After some drinks
& touching
          she said
"It's hard to get into a poem,
isn't it."

ANSWER

It's not
a final shape

or a puzzle
that won't fit;

two girls there
at the window

saying in unison,
& pointing at the other,

I'm for
laughing & she's
for bed, but we
don't go together.

Only the ground
is dark
where you can't see it

New York City
June 1970

26

FIRST THOUGHT WHEN COMING THROUGH THE DOOR AFTER BEING OUT ALL NIGHT

Hey, I must be home.
Everyone's sleeping

HE WAS HEAVY WEIGHT

He was heavy weight
against her.
She was heavy weight
against him.
Mercy was nonexistent.

Bird pecks on
window ledge;
startles him/
her.

Lightning/Thunder
threatens obedience;
lie/lay still.

When he/she was
sensual: mind's eye
open

The body is
            every-
thing excepting
the mind;

Instinct comes
first. Intellect
follows, develops
from there

depending

Found: scrap of
paper by their
son. Reads, Be a Big
Song to Yourself
page 45. Happy Love

SECRET POEM #1

Who was this young girl
coming to me in a dream,
asking me to look at her
when I was flat on my back;
promising I would never forget her,
and awoke making love to all my poems

AFTER TALKING WITH A POET
WHEN HE'D BEEN OUT OF JAIL FOR A WEEK

What is real
works out/
again;
brings me out
now; that sight
given me; again:

Live; or/
on a borrowed
record player;

with some booze
bought, begged, stole,

or traded in on;
I look up
holding on this way

PERSONAL POEM #2
                for *Norma*

It's great going around this way /nude/
and being all there
with all of you there:
in the bed all to ourselves

In a dream I dreamed that while dreaming
a dream about a green fiddler
dancing in my ear telling me this
while I was ducking and dodging
old nightmares come back

Believing him when I awoke in you
working hard for Hope, Firm Ground

32

TONIGHT

Tonight I am
looking all over
you
and don't know what
to do about it

FINDING OUT

The heat in your crotch
should be worth knowing
where you are now,
and not intended
for 'natural impulse.'

POET

Clams live in the muck
under the ocean, but we
eat them as a delicacy.
What can I tell you then
fat girl trying to get me
into your bed: that I'm
not up to delicacies tonight?

LIBRARY

The local library key
to the bathroom
                has MEN
scotch taped to it
on thin, white paper

POEM
   for Jean Larson

She sings
with tender loving care
knowing everything
is absurd
except love;
lying down with it
in common testament:

creating

ALMOST

Before you married
you almost made it
with me, standing

in your living
room coming out
of your swimming

suit: the sun's sweat
still coming out
of you against my palm

sliding over your breast
to your nipple rising,
getting hard: almost

there; shaking off old
ghosts without knowing
it: almost knowing the *I*

is first: almost having it
all: in the living
room. Without charge.

Free & Clear. Until
you said there wasn't
time and left

to get a laundered towel
and meet your obligation
after you dressed.

FOR AWHILE
            for Rida

You are
afraid. Coming around
from before. Where
did you start
putting yourself to-
gether at; all the time
trying: you had it.
No one knew. Time
brought us together,
helping for awhile:
undressing by
the big soft bed

GETTING THERE

The way
you make me

feel: I want to see
what you look

like. The grass is
new and damp. Next

time, there

WHAT LEROY ONCE SAID TO HIS WIFE
AND THEN TOLD ME

So much
to do; the
head, the damn
head; a probable
dream means only
it has happened: gone
to you.

INSIDE AND OUT

Too much inside
myself the I
stands out; the

hand on the
door-knob opens,
closes the door.

The boots in, out
of the sand continue
to move, carry me;

comforted that the wind
holds, does not necessarily
challenge. I sit down

somewhere. The sea
is flat; waves by name
only. Both separate.

Not this, is where
I am. Some enthusiasms
have vanished.

The move of
the hand to
find the sand

BIBLE CAMP

Redemption for being
there is found

at dawn in the
woods with a girl

who makes you feel
like it's worth it:

becoming a man
in her wetness

THE FRIENDS
for Bob McCullough

In a pasture,
on a log
by a creek, drinking
old carrot wine;
getting high
talking love up
against the sunshine

ONE FOR AUDREY

The candle burned
out while I was
sleeping tonight,
but you weren't
there anyway

WHERE TO

Where to
is not love
necessarily,
in the direction.
I don't
want to die
like this

ARGUMENT FOR LOVE

1

There's just you and me
Where are you now?

2

UP

&

DOWN

OVER

&

AROUND

The act in your skull goes on

from   time:

WHEN?

0   to   29
    to   16   to six
            to   17
                to   12   to
                            21

etcetera, etcetera, which means

> what-
> ever
> you
> want
> it
> to
> mean

depending upon what love means to you.

3

Here's your chance
I'm undressing you
for me & you & us
do it back to me for you &
me & us: FREE & CLEAR
loving from inside *I*
out   to you

4

Why do you re-act this way?
Emotion inside

5

standing without support
except   except   except

WHAT?

6

My shoes are off
my feet are cold
been to hell
twice   really

I've a right to ask

OHOHOH pity him, brother OHOHOH
pity him, brother OHOHOH

who chants now
Black   White
            Both

                    FUCK YOU!

whose ever uncle you are. It's too easy
to be stoic. I've been there too; part
of the great american way. You never went
far enough. Integrity is buried deep in
hell brother.

to bring it into focus
the sweat & moaning
that makes it right
between us

                    I see it

would make it right

if you could/would. Unlikely.
                    One can't
                    carry it
                    indefinitely

                    8

her: "You sweat so much
     how come you scratch?"

                    9

 me: "I'm an animal."

No room for lovers sweet talk here

                    10

                    yet

                    11

                    Discipline

                    12

My hands love you
feeling you draw plans
on your body's curve
against me
          for your next move

Where are you now

OHOHOH   I've got to laugh here

me: "How do I fuck you right?"
her: "That's no way to talk, silly."

me: "You hid your crucifix again"
her: "It's wrong this way"
me: "I know"

"Let's start again," I say
getting out of bed. "Dress.
You do it to me."

what for?

[small voice inside of me
take a chance]
"Ok, for love."

You're crazy.

"Ok, but let's start
again."

I can't

"Good-bye."

Where are you going?

"Out to start again."

17

Me, yelling
down the street:

Which way is it?

All of'um say
All of'um say

come find me
if you can

18

KNOCK KNOCK

Come in, she says
meaning open the door

19

I do
for me & you
& love

even if I can't say it

20

yet

OPEN
> *for Darrell Gray*

Is the pain
of my life in the spaces
between these words,
my text, myself

HOPE

In me, somewhere,
this Christmas 1969,
if I can,
a girl walking
in clean, white snow

POEM FOR MYSELF

Love them all but keep a home
in your mind: I hold my son's hand
when I'm climbing stairs.
Sweet breath of clarity

SPRING FLOWER
4 MAY 1970
For My Son Saroyan

*In Tribute to the 4 Students
Killed at Kent State University*

3½ now
& handed me,
his father,
Poet
for most of my
life
at age 31 &
almost a half,
a bright yellow
tulip
sometime
this afternoon.

Said the tulip should,
without words,
after filling
a glass jar
with water,
be in the water
& put on
my writing table

where

we watched
it bend,
then lean into,
three days later,
stalks of
broom straw flowers:

Opening

& closing there
against
& around
them.

Likely,
in similarity,
the reason
Poets don't begin
their poems
with,
I know why

East Falmouth, Mass.
9 May 1970

ARGUMENT FOR LOVE

"I think Humphrey's stuff is getting it, getting
the idea, getting to the idea---that living is the
first poem, and getting that understood in simple
true words is the second."--*William Saroyan*

"What I like most about James Humphrey's poems is
their unflinching honesty. They are "arguments"
for preserving in life that which make us most human
a disarming simplicity of diction, plain and hard
meaning without descriptive qualification, reverber-
ates in the highly charged condensation of these poe
His is the language in which men dream of what their
lives ought to be. Again and again, I come back
to these poems. They reassure me that a direct and
true language is still possible in this tortured
and confused world. I flatter myself to call him
my contemporary."--*Darrell Gray*

"James Humphrey's poems are deceptive in the way
icebergs are. Their short lines and apparently
simple language mask a depth and mass of feeling
which are forcefully there beneath and beyond
surface statement. Again and again, in reading
these poems, one is struck by their ramifications,
as though in the white spaces surrounding his words
Humphrey had stationed many voices, each with its
own resonant intimation of the world."
                                    --*Brendan Galvin*

"They are direct, honest, and personal, which is
the best thing about the whole current direction
in poetry."--*Andrew Glaze*

Cover photo/Dan Gerber
Cover design/James Humphrey